Spiders

Trudi Strain Trueit

Marshall Cavendish
Benchmark
New York

Published by Marshall Cavendish Benchmark
An imprint of Marshall Cavendish Corporation

Other Marshall Cavendish Offices:
Marshall Cavendish International (Asia) Private Limited, 1 New Industrial Road, Singapore 536196
Marshall Cavendish International (Thailand) Co. Ltd. 253 Asoke, 12th Flr, Sukhumvit 21 Road, Klongtoey Nua, Wattana, Bangkok 10110, Thailand
Marshall Cavendish (Malaysia) Sdn Bhd, Times Subang, Lot 46, Subang Hi-Tech Industrial Park, Batu Tiga, 40000 Shah Alam, Selangor Darul Ehsan, Malaysia

Marshall Cavendish is a trademark of Times Publishing Limited

Library of Congress Cataloging-in-Publication Data

Trueit, Trudi Strain.
Spiders / by Trudi Strain Trueit.
p. cm. — (Backyard safari)
Includes bibliographical references and index.
Summary: "Identify specific spiders. Explore their behavior, life cycle, mating habits,
geographical location, anatomy, enemies, and defenses"—Provided by publisher.
ISBN 978-1-60870-249-7 (print)   ISBN 978-1-60870-628-0 (ebook)
1. Spiders—Juvenile literature. 2. Spiders—Identification—Juvenile literature. I. Title.
QL458.4.T83 2012
595.4'4—dc22
2010030335

Editor: Christine Florie
Publisher: Michelle Bisson
Art Director: Anahid Hamparian
Series Designer: Alicia Mikles

Expert Reader: Dr. Linda S. Rayor, Department of Entomology, Cornell University, Ithaca, New York

Photo research by Marybeth Kavanagh

Cover photo by Cusp/SuperStock
The photographs in this book are used by permission and through the courtesy of: *SuperStock*: 5, 9; IndexStock, 4, 28; James Urbach, 6; Science Faction, 8; Imagebroker.net, 10; age fotostock, 11, 15, 20 (lower right), 22 (bottom); F1 ONLINE, 14; All Canada Photos, 20 (top left); *Alamy*: Image Quest Marine, 7; John T. Fowler, 20 (top right); Peter Arnold, Inc., 22 (top left); Michael Mules, 23 (top right); Nigel Cattlin, 23 (bottom); Emilio Ereza, 25; *Minden Pictures*: Steve Packham/npl, 12; Stephen Dalton, 21 (bottom); Rolf Nussbaumer/npl, 23 (top left); *Media Bakery*: BigStockPhoto, 12 (cap), 12 (glasses); *Cutcaster*: Sergey Skryl, 12 (camera); Sergej Razvodovskij, 12 (pencils); Marek Kosmal, 12 (magnifier); *The Image Works*: Charles O. Cecil, 19; *Animals Animals*: Bill Beatty, 20 (lower left); *Getty Images*: Steve Maslowski/Visuals Unlimited, 21 (top left); *Photo Researchers, Inc.*: Camazine/K. Visscher, 21 (top right); Stephen P. Parker, 22 (top right); *US Fish & Wildlife Service*: Gordon Smith, 24

Printed in Malaysia (T)
1 3 5 6 4 2

5656 1359 4/15

Contents

Introduction

Have you ever watched baby spiders hatch from a silky egg sac? Or seen a butterfly sip nectar from a flower? If you have, you know how wonderful it is to discover nature for yourself. Each book in the Backyard Safari series takes you step-by-step on an easy outdoor adventure, then helps you identify the animals you've found. You'll also learn ways to attract, observe, and protect these valuable creatures. As you read, be on the lookout for the Safari Tips and Trek Talk facts sprinkled throughout the book. Ready? The fun starts just steps from your back door!

ONE
A Spinning World

Spiders are mysterious, clever, and a little bit creepy. Some are as big as a dinner plate, but most are smaller than your fingernail. Despite their size, these creatures have extraordinary survival skills and abilities. Spiders have lived on Earth for more than 160 million years. You can find them resting under desert rocks, scurrying across mountain wildflowers, and of course, crafting webs in your backyard.

Garden spiders weave orb webs, which look like wheels with spokes.

Trek Talk
Scientists have identified more than 40,000 types of spiders in the world but say there are tens of thousands more yet to be discovered.

Acrobatic Arachnids

Spiders may hang out in your yard with ants, ladybugs, and other insects, but they are not insects. They belong to a group of animals called **arachnids** (uh-RACK-nids). Spiders are related to scorpions, mites, ticks, and harvestmen (sometimes referred to as daddy longlegs). Spiders have two body segments (insects have three) and eight legs (insects have six). Unlike many insects, spiders do not have antennae or wings.

Safari Tip

With their long, spindly legs, harvestmen (daddy longlegs) are easy to spot. But don't confuse them with spiders. They are distant cousins. Harvestmen have one body part, not two, and two eyes instead of eight. Like spiders, they have **chelicerae** (kuh-LISS-er-ee), a pair of fanged front jaws, but they do not have venom. Also, harvestmen do not spin webs but instead hunt at night for tiny insects such as aphids and pill bugs.

A spider's head and thorax are joined to form its front body segment, or **cephalothorax** (sef-uh-loh-THAWR-aks). A spider's eyes, mouth, and legs are located on the cephalothorax. Most spiders have eight eyes. While some spiders see only light and dark, others, such as jumping spiders, have excellent vision. A spider's eight legs are covered in tiny hairs or scales that are sensitive to touch and motion. The hairs are so sensitive they can pick up vibrations in the air, such as a moth flying by.

When an insect gets stuck in a spider's web, the spider instantly feels the vibration. It scurries across its web to grab the **prey**.

Spiders have multiple eyes. How many does this jumping spider have?

To do this, it uses its chelicerae and **pedipalps**, two antennaelike limbs located below the chelicerae. Sometimes, but not always, a spider will wrap its prey in silk. Next, the spider bites the insect with its hollow fangs, releasing venom. Its mouthparts release digestive juices into the prey, turning the organs to liquid. The spider then sucks out the liquid for nutrients. Backyard spiders typically eat insects and other spiders.

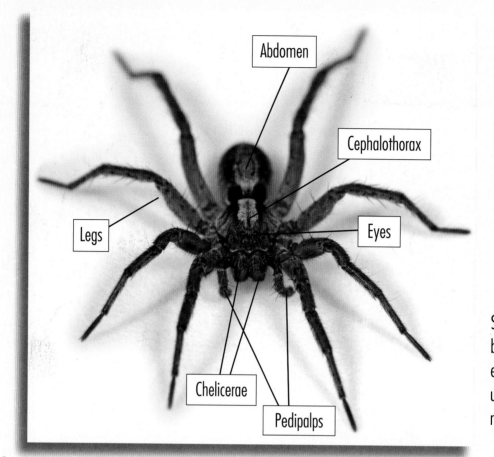

Abdomen

Cephalothorax

Legs

Eyes

Chelicerae

Pedipalps

Spiders have two body segments, eight legs, and usually, two or more eyes.

A spider's second body segment, the **abdomen**, contains two or three pairs of **spinnerets**. These glands spin silk from proteins made in the abdomen. (It's still a mystery to scientists how spiders form silk.) Spigots release the strands, which are wound together to make fiber. Spider silk is incredibly strong. It's also quite flexible and may stretch up to two hundred times its length! Nearly all spiders trail a silky thread, or **dragline**, behind them. It acts as a safety line, allowing the spider to quickly drop or climb. Silk is also used to attract a mate, create an egg sac, line a burrow, and build a web.

Along Came a Spider

Although many spiders spin webs, some have other ways of catching a meal. Jumping spiders rely on excellent vision to help them leap on passing prey. They can pounce more than a foot (forty times their body length)! The bolas spider lures in male moths by producing a chemical mimicking the odors made by the female moth. When the moth gets close, the bolas tosses out a silky thread with a sticky button at the end to catch the insect. Crab spiders (named for the way they move sideways like crabs), use **camouflage** to capture prey. A crab spider (above) will change its body color from white to yellow to better match a flower. It waits on the blossom for a bee or a fly to land, then attacks.

Threads of Life

Male spiders are often smaller than females. In some species, the male is one thousand times smaller than the female. When a male orb weaver spider finds a female of his own kind, he may attach a special thread to her web and then pluck it to get her attention.

Each type of spider drums its own rhythm. Vibration plays an important role in spider courtship. Even spiders that don't spin webs use vibrations to find one another.

A female spider lays from a handful to several thousand eggs in an egg sac she makes from her silk. Many spiders attach their egg sacs to twigs, plants, or a web. Some females leave the egg sac. Others, like the green lynx spider, guard it until the **spiderlings** are born. The eggs may hatch after a few weeks or the following spring. A female wolf spider carries the spiderlings around on her back until they are old enough to survive on their own.

Trek Talk

Young spiders may release long strands of silk and use them like kite tails to ride the winds to other places. This is called ballooning. Ballooning spiders may travel to great heights or long distances.

Arachnids have a hard outer covering called an **exoskeleton**. To grow, a spider must molt, or shed, this exoskeleton. Each time a spider grows, it splits the hard outer shell and wriggles free. Spiders molt four to twelve times before becoming adults. Most backyard spiders live from a few months up to a year, but others, like tarantulas, may live up to twenty-five years!

Now that you've explored the incredible world of spiders, it's time to find them!

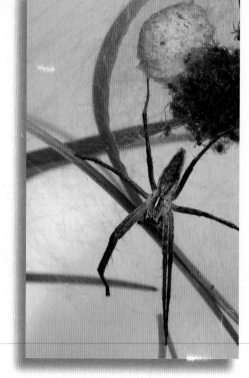

A female nursery spider attends her young as they emerge from her egg sac.

TWO

You Are the Explorer

In North America, the best seasons to go on safari for spiders are spring, summer, and fall. If outdoor temperatures stay above 50 degrees Fahrenheit in winter where you live, you may be able to spot them year-round. Choose a day when it isn't windy or rainy, and the temperature is above 60 °F. Try going out early on a cool, misty morning, when spiderwebs are often covered in dew and much easier to see (see Chapter Four to learn more about web hunting).

Safari Tip

Do you see a spiderweb with a thick, zigzagging ribbon of silk? No one knows exactly why spiders sometimes add this ribbon, called a **stabilimentum**. It may be used to camouflage the spider from predators, lure insects, keep birds from flying into the web, or shade the spider from the sun— or perhaps it does all these things!

What Do I Wear?

- A hat with a brim
- A long-sleeved shirt
- Jeans or long pants
- Sunglasses
- Sunscreen

What Do I Take?

- Magnifying glass
- Digital camera
- Notebook
- Colored pens or pencils
- Water to drink

Trek Talk

Ants are distasteful to birds, so many spiders do their best to copy them. The ant-mimic jumper (right) not only looks like an ant but will walk on six legs and wave its two front legs like antennae!

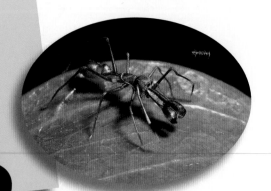

Where Do I Go?

Spiders will be most attracted to these things in your backyard:

- ❋ Grass
- ❋ Flowers
- ❋ Bushes
- ❋ Trees, stumps, and logs
- ❋ Rocks, stepping stones, and loose pavers
- ❋ Porches, fences, and decks
- ❋ Windowsills

If your backyard doesn't offer these features, here are some other safari locations you can try:

- ❋ Woodlands
- ❋ Fields
- ❋ Garden nurseries
- ❋ Public parks

Always have an adult with you if you are going beyond your backyard.

Webbed Wonders

Many backyard spiders weave an orb, a spiral-shaped web that looks like a wheel with spokes (below). Orb weavers, such as the black-and-yellow garden spider, tend to make a new web every day (often in the evening). First, a spider eats its old web, recycling almost all the silk. It then replaces the spokes. Spokes are what give the web its strength. Next, the spider attaches a fresh, sticky spiral. The spiral acts like elastic. When an insect hits the web, the spirals stretch to absorb the impact. It takes less than an hour for the spider to weave a new web. To do so, the spider produces up to 70 feet of silk!

As you safari, here are more types of webs to watch for:

Cobwebs: thick tangles of silk with no set pattern (black widow, common house spider)

Irregular webs: thin, oddly shaped webs spun at an angle in a corner (cellar spider)

Sheet webs: thick flat or bowl-shaped webs, often with attached hiding tunnels (grass spider, doily weaver, hammock spider)

What Do I Do?

✳ Begin your safari by searching for spiderwebs. Spiders prefer to build their webs where they can be easily attached and are protected from the rain. You might find one draped on a bush, another strung under a deck rail, and still another tucked in the corner of a porch.

✳ If you discover an empty web, its creator is probably not far. Take a careful look around, or come back in a bit to see if the spider has returned. Often spiders attach lines to rolled leaves near the web, allowing them to run back to the web when an insect gets caught. Follow the lines to see if you can locate a spider. If you open a rolled leaf, the spider is likely to run back onto its web.

✳ Use your magnifying glass. Search windowsills, fences, decks, and patios. Check shrubs, leafy plants, and the grass. Peek under small logs, flat rocks, and stepping-stones. Look inside or under flower blossoms to find camouflaged crab spiders. Spiders are everywhere!

While on safari, use your magnifying glass to search for spiders that may be on plants and shrubs.

Safari Tip

Spiders don't attack people. They bite humans only when they're scared, which is why it isn't a good idea to handle them. Spider venom is usually harmless. Still, bites may hurt, become itchy or infected, or be slow to heal. The poison of the black widow and the brown recluse may cause nausea, muscle aches, and occasionally death. Did you know the bite of North America's largest spider, the tarantula, is painful but no more dangerous than a bee sting? You will want to beware, however, of its hairs. Touching your face after handling a tarantula's bristling hairs may irritate your eyes, nose, and mouth.

❋ When you discover a spider, move slowly. Most backyard spiders scurry away when they sense danger. Do not touch or handle a spider.

❋ Snap a photo or draw a sketch of your spider. Make an entry in your notebook, too. Look at the spider's abdomen first. Is it oval, round, or long? What color is it? Does the abdomen have any **field marks**, such as blotches, stripes, or other patterns? How about the spider's legs? Are they long or short? Also, if your spider has a web, describe it. Note where you found your spider and what it was doing. Leave a blank line at the bottom of your entry to add its name later.

SPIDER

Abdomen: oval shape, black and yellow stripes

Field marks: yellow spots on abdomen

Legs: long, black with yellow stripes

Web: orb with stabilimentum

Location: found between rose bushes near back fence

Activity: spider sitting in center of web

Name: _____

Your Drawing or Photo Goes Here

* Spend about a half hour to an hour on safari (don't forget to drink your water).
* Clean up the area, and take all your belongings with you when you leave.

Did you see many spiders on your safari? If so, good work. If not, don't get discouraged. Every safari offers something different to see. Try again soon. Next time, why not try a night safari? Turn on your porch light to attract insects. Watch to see what type of night-active spiders come to hunt them. At home, download your photos onto the computer and print them. It's time to identify your discoveries!

THREE

A Guide to Spiders

Your arachnid adventure is finished, and you're ready to identify the spiders you've found. Here's what to do: select an entry from your notebook. If you took a photo, paste it next to its description. As you compare your entry with the photos on pages 20–23, focus on these major areas:

❋ Abdomen: shape, color, and field marks (spots, stripes, blotches)

❋ Legs: color and length

❋ Web: Did your spider have one? If so, what type was it? The photos in the field guide are arranged based on spiders' web-weaving habits. This way, even if you aren't able to make a match you may still be able to tell which group your spider belongs to:

> ❋ orb weavers
>
> ❋ irregular-web and cobweb weavers
>
> ❋ sheet-web and funnel-web weavers
>
> ❋ non-web weavers

If you find your spider, congratulations! Write its name in the space you left in your notebook. If you can only narrow in on your spider's family, though, that's okay, too. If you don't see your spider or its family, don't worry. North America is home to more than 3,400 types of spiders—far too many to picture here. Use the resources in the Find Out More section for further help with spider identification.

SPIDER

Abdomen: oval shape, black and yellow stripes

Field marks: yellow spots on abdomen

Legs: long, black with yellow stripes

Web: orb with stabilimentum

Location: found between rose bushes near back fence

Activity: spider sitting in center of web

Name: black-and-yellow garden spider

Spider Guide:
Orb Weavers

Banded Garden Spider

Marbled Orb Weaver

Shamrock Orb Weave

Silver Garden Spider

Spider Guide:
Irregular-web and Cobweb Weavers

Black Widow Spider

Brown Recluse Spider

House Spider

Spider Guide:
Sheet-web and Funnel-web Weavers

Grass Spider

Hammock Spider

Nursery Web Spider

Spider Guide:
Non-web Weavers

Bold Jumping Spider

Giant Wolf Spider

Goldenrod Crab Spider

FOUR
Try This!
Projects You Can Do

Did you know spiders dine on more than 200 trillion mosquitoes, flies, and other insects every year? Spiders are the number-one **predator** of insects on Earth. Without them, the world would be overrun with insects that spread disease, harm trees and plants, and destroy crops.

Why not help protect spiders by welcoming them to your backyard? They'll return the favor by keeping your insect population under control and giving you plenty of action to observe. Here are some fun, simple ways to attract and watch these helpful arachnids.

Saving Spiders

Wolf spiders are named for the way they chase down their prey. They measure up to 4 inches long (including legs) and live in underground burrows. Although wolf spiders are abundant throughout North America, one type is at risk. Discovered in 1971, the Kauai cave wolf spider (above) is found only in lava tubes and caves on the island of Kauai in Hawaii. While most wolf spiders have eight eyes, the Kauai cave wolf spider has no eyes at all. It doesn't need them. Living in near-total darkness, the spider hunts by smell, not sight. Habitat destruction, pollution, and chemicals threaten the Kauai cave wolf spider. The U.S. Fish and Wildlife Service is working to preserve Kauai's caves in hopes of saving these rare spiders from **extinction**.

Spider Garden

Plant a summer garden to attract beneficial spiders. Choose six to eight plants from the Spider Favorites list on page 26. Pick a spot for your garden that is sheltered from the wind. Use good soil. Water the plants every few days. Don't use pesticides. They will kill spiders as well as the insects spiders dine on. Spend at least ten minutes in your garden twice a week observing spider behavior. Take photos and write in your journal about what you see. In the fall, don't remove the dead plants or blossoms, or you'll destroy egg sacs. With any luck, you will have a new generation of spiders to observe the following spring!

Summer gardens attract spiders and are good places to observe them.

Spiders Favorites Plant List

FLOWERS	HERBS
Rose	Dill
Cosmos	Spearmint
Marigold	Fennel
Daisy	Yarrow
Tulip	Parsley
Lily	Chives

Web Hunt

Have you ever gone outside on a cool morning and seen glittering spiderwebs everywhere? Tiny drops of water clinging to the silky threads can make these nearly invisible works of art suddenly very noticeable. Dewy mornings are perfect for a web hunt. Take your magnifying glass, notebook, and camera with you. The dewdrops will help you to see, and better understand, the structure of a web. The average orb web has about 1,500 connections!

Take photographs and make entries in your notebook about the webs you observe. Do any have stabilimenta? Also, try going on a web hunt at different times of the day. In the early evening, you might get to see a spider taking apart its old web and weaving a new one.

Trek Talk

According to Guinness World Records, the common house spider takes top honors for having the strongest web. In one recorded instance, a mouse was found trapped in the web!

Spider Nursery

In early summer, find a spider's egg sac in your garden. Take a photograph and make an entry in your notebook describing it. Call the entry "Spider Nursery," and include the date. Is there a female spider nearby guarding the sac? Can you identify her? Come back every few days as you wait for the spiderlings to be born (at most, this should take a few weeks). When the spiderlings hatch, watch how they behave. Do they remain in the egg sac or cluster together outside of it? What happens to the

If you find an egg sac, like the one above, you can watch for spiderlings to emerge.

young spiders one week after birth? How about one month? Keep notes in your journal as you watch life in the spider nursery progress.

We see spiders so frequently it can be easy to take them for granted—especially when you accidentally stumble through a sticky web. Yet their beautiful colors, remarkable talents, and clever tactics remind us that these tiny backyard creatures are anything but ordinary. Now that you know their secrets, you can safari for spiders any time. How about today?

Glossary

abdomen	the second body segment of a spider, containing the spinnerets
arachnids	a group of animals, including spiders, scorpions, and harvestmen, with two main body sections and eight legs
camouflage	to use color as a disguise
cephalothorax	the first body segment of a spider, containing the eyes, mouth, and legs
chelicerae	a spider's fang-tipped jaws
dragline	a safety line of silk
exoskeleton	a spider's hard outer covering, which acts as a skeleton
extinction	the dying out of a particular type of animal or plant
field marks	spots, stripes, or other distinguishing marks on an animal
pedipalps	two fingerlike appendages that help a spider catch, hold, and crush prey
predator	an animal that hunts another animal for food
prey	an animal that is hunted for food
spiderlings	young spiders
spinnerets	a spider's silk-spinning glands
stabilimentum	a thick ribbon of silk an orb weaver spider sometimes adds to its web

Find Out More

Books

Evans, Arthur V. *National Wildlife Federation Field Guide to Insects and Spiders of North America*. New York: Sterling Publishing Group, 2007.

Jackson, Tom. *Spiders*. Danbury, CT: Scholastic, 2008.

McGavin, George. *Amazing Insects and Spiders*. Pleasantville, NY: Gareth Stevens, 2008.

DVDs

Biology: Mini World of Insects and Spiders. TMW Media Group, 2008.

Spiders: Backyard Science. Phoenix Learning Group, 2008.

Websites

BioKIDS Critter Catalog: Spiders

www.biokids.umich.edu/critters/Araneae/

Explore the world of crab spiders, cellar spiders, and other backyard arachnids at this educational website. Use the photo gallery to help identify your spiders.

eNature Field Guide

www.enature.com/fieldguides

Log on to this online field guide, then click on "spiders" to see photos, read descriptions, and learn fun facts about familiar backyard spiders.

National Geographic

http://animals.nationalgeographic.com/animals/bugs.html

Discover the truth about the black widow spider, get a close-up view of a spider exoskeleton, and see video of a jumping spider in action.

Index

Page numbers in **boldface** are illustrations.

About the Author

As a child, **TRUDI STRAIN TRUEIT** could often be found searching her backyard for spiders, beetles, butterflies, and other wildlife. As an adult, she has written more than fifty nonfiction books for young readers, covering such topics as weather, wildlife, and earth science. She is the author of four other books in the Backyard Safari series, including *Birds, Frogs and Toads,* and *Squirrels.* Trueit has a B.A. in broadcast journalism. She lives in Everett, Washington, with her husband, Bill, a high school photography teacher. Visit her website at www.truditrueit.com.